MW01715739

Grandpa, Tell us about your life

Grandpa, Tell us about your life

A Grandfather's Guided Memory Book
and Family Keepsake Journal

by Rachel Hutcheson

ISBN: 978-1-7329611-6-6

www.rachelhutchesonwriter.com

This Book Belongs To

____

Contents

How To Use This Journal - 7

The Beginning - 9

Childhood - 19

School Days and Interests - 31

Work and Play - 43

Love, Fatherhood, Grandpa -53

Beliefs and Values -73

Thoughts and Wise Words -81

Quick Fun Questions - 89

How To Use This Journal

This journal is filled with questions and prompts to help you share your stories, thoughts, and memories with your family.

Some of the questions ask for your advice. Others ask about a favorite memory or what you liked most about a time or event.

To start, flip through the book to see what is inside.

When answering the questions, write as much or as little as you like. Then go back and write more if you choose.

The more details you give, the more your family will learn about you and your life.

You will find extra blank note pages at the end of each chapter. Use them to add to your answers if you need more space or for additional thoughts and memories.

Answer the questions in any order you like.

Most importantly, enjoy your trip down memory lane. It is a journey through happy times and the wisdom you have gained. And it is a keepsake for your family and future generations.

The Beginning

You can stay young as long as you learn.

-Emily Dickinson

Name at Birth:

Date of Birth:

City and State:

Weight:

Length:

Mother's Birth Name:

Mother's Age:

Father's Birth Name:

Father's Age:

Were you born in a hospital? At home? A car?

What story were you told about your birth?

Were you told you were a sweet or fussy baby? Did you sleep through the night?

Do you still have toys, blankets, or other memorabilia from your early years?

Where was your first home? How long did you live there?

Were you named after anyone? Who?

Do you have any nicknames? Who gave them to you?

How old were you when you started to walk?

Do you remember learning how to tie your shoes or to tell time? What do you remember about it?

Do you have any siblings? Write down their names and when they were born.

What are your earliest memories?

What are your grandparent's names? When and where were they born?

Did you spend time with your grandparents when you were growing up? What do you remember most about those times?

Attach your baby picture here.

Use this space to share more stories about your birth, parents, and younger days.

Childhood

The most interesting information comes from children,

for they tell all they know and then stop.

-Mark Twain

What do you remember about your childhood home? Did you have a yard? A swing set?

Did you have your own bedroom? Did you share? With whom? What did your room look like?

Who was your best friend when you were a kid? What do you remember doing together?

Did your family celebrate birthdays? How? What kind of birthday cake did you like?

Did you see Santa? Do you remember asking him for anything special?

What were your favorite cartoons or comics?

What did you want to be when you grew up?

What chores did you have at home?

Did you get an allowance? How much?

Did you save or spend your money? What would you buy?

Do you remember reading or having a favorite book read to you during childhood? What was it?

Did you have any pets? What kinds? What were their names?

What was your favorite holiday? What did you like most about it?

Were there lots of kids in your neighborhood? Did everyone play together? What games did you play?

Did your family take any vacations or visit relatives? What memories stick in your mind about those times?

Did you have a bike? What kind? What color?

What was your favorite family meal? Who made it?

What was your favorite candy?

What were you most interested in as a child? What did you love to do?

How did you spend your summer days during elementary school?

Did you ever go to camp or on a retreat? Where did you go? What was it like?

Write down a favorite childhood memory.

What is the best advice your parents gave you during childhood?

Use this space to share more stories and thoughts about your childhood.

School Days and Interests

Jump, and you will find out how

to unfold your wings as you fall.

-Ray Bradbury

What schools did you attend? List the names and cities.

Did you walk to school? How far?

Did you have a teacher who inspired you? What did they teach? What made them great?

What subjects did you like the most in school?

How would you describe yourself as a teenager?

What style of clothes did you wear in junior high/middle school and high school?

What kind of music did you like?

What was one of your favorite songs?

Did you participate in any extracurricular activities in school? Such as sports, clubs, choir, band, or others?

What school years did you enjoy the most? Why?

Write down a happy memory from your school days.

Where is the first place you drove after getting your driver's license?

Did you belong to organizations such as scouting, a church, 4-H, or a club outside of school? Which ones?

Did you go to any school dances? What do you remember about them?

Did you take any school trips? Where did you go?

What did you and your friends do for fun in high school? College?

Who were your closest friends during your school days? Are you still in touch with them?

What are the most valuable things you learned in school?

If you could go back and study anything you wanted-what classes would you take?

What advice do you have about school and education?

Use this space to share more memories and thoughts about your school days and interests.

Work and Play

Keep your face always toward the

sunshine – and shadows will fall behind you.

-Walt Whitman

What was your first job?

How much were you paid?

What other work have you done? List all the jobs you can remember.

Which job has been your favorite? Why?

What was the worst job you ever had?

What is something unusual that happened at work?

What do you think makes a person successful in their career?

What are you most proud of regarding your work life?

If you had the chance, is there any other career you would like to try?

Do you have any hobbies? What are they?

What are some of your favorite movies?

Do you collect anything? What?

What is the craziest thing you have ever bought?

Are you a sports fan? What teams do you like?

Have you done any traveling? What places have you enjoyed the most? Why?

Name five things you would like to see in the world.

What amazes you about life?

What is something you have always wanted to have?

What do you like to do for entertainment?

What is something interesting that most people don't know about you?

Use this space to share more stories and thoughts about your work, hobbies, and life.

Love, Fatherhood, Grandpa

I think of love, and you,

and my heart grows full and warm…

-Emily Dickinson

Love

What is your spouse's/partner's name and date of birth?

How did you meet?

Did you know right away they were the one for you? What was your first impression?

Where did you go on your first date?

What is the sweetest thing your spouse has done for you?

When did you know you were in love?

Was there a proposal? Describe it.

Where did you live when you were first married?

What are the best things about marriage?

Write about a fun trip you took together.

Write about an adventure you had together.

Fatherhood

What did becoming a Dad mean to you?

What did you think when you saw your baby/babies for the first time?

Attach a picture of your children here.

What are your children's names and dates of birth?

Are your children named after anyone? Who?

What is the best part of babyhood?

Is there a song you sang to your children when they were babies? What was it?

How did you change when you became a dad?

How has being a dad changed the way you look at the world?

What is something simple and fun you did with your kids when they were young?

How would you describe each of your children?

Write down a special memory you have of each of your children.

What has been your biggest surprise about fatherhood?

What is your favorite name for dad? (dad, pop, etc.)

Do you remember being excited about a gift you bought for your kids? What was it?

Did you ever take your family for a Sunday drive? Where would you go?

What is the hardest part of being a dad?

What is the best part of being a dad?

What family tradition have you continued from your parents?

Write down a favorite holiday memory.

Write about a fun family vacation memory.

What did you learn from your parents about parenthood?

Grandpa

What was the first thing you did when you found out you were going to be a grandpa?

What is the best thing about being a grandpa?

What do you love to hear your grandkids say?

What hopes and dreams do you have for your grandchildren?

Write down a happy memory you have of your grandkids.

Attach a picture of your grandchildren here.

Use this space to share more memories about love and family.

Beliefs and Values

To be yourself in a world that is constantly trying to make you something else is the greatest accomplishment.

-Ralph Waldo Emerson

What is most important to you?

What could you do without and still be happy?

Do you believe in a higher power?

Do you believe in an afterlife? What do you think the afterlife is?

What has improved about the world since you were a kid?

What was better about the world when you were a kid?

What values do you try to live by?

What dreams do you have for the future?

What has made you a stronger person?

What characteristics do you admire in people?

What words of encouragement do you have for someone who wants to give up on something?

Use the space below to share more stories and thoughts about your beliefs and values.

Thoughts and Wise Words

Knowledge comes, but wisdom lingers.

-Alfred Lord Tennyson

What do you like about getting older?

What do you not like about getting older?

What do couples need to do to make a marriage or relationship work?

What are three simple things a person can do to help others?

What do you know now that you wish you had known when you were younger?

They say the best things in life are free. What are the best free things in life?

Do you have a life philosophy? What is it?

Do you have any money advice?

What have you learned from your kids about life?

What things are a waste of time?

What are three things a person should do while they are young?

What is a good lesson you learned from personal experience?

What advice do you have for creating a happy life?

What is the best advice you have received about life?

Do you have a bucket list? What kinds of things are on it?

Use this space to share more stories and thoughts on life and good living.

Quick Fun Questions

Wealth is the ability to fully experience life.

-Henry David Thoreau

Have You Ever?

Have you ever ridden a motorcycle?

Have you ever written or memorized a poem? Write it down if you remember it. (You can also add it to the notes at the back of the book.)

Have you ever traveled to a foreign country? Which ones?

Have you ever known someone who lived to be one hundred years old? Who?

Have you ever achieved a personal goal you really wanted to achieve? What was it?

Have you ever learned to do something you never thought you could do? What was it?

Have you ever been to a circus? Which one?

Have you ever camped in a tent? Where?

Have you ever changed a flat tire on a car? A bike?

Have you ever run for a public office in or out of school? What office?

Have you ever planted a flower or a vegetable garden?

Have you ever painted a room or a house?

Have you ever run out of gas? Where?

Have you ever owned your own business? What business?

Have you ever been to New York City? What did you think?

Have you ever eaten a banana split?

Have you ever put your foot in an ocean? Which one?

Have you ever danced like no one was watching?

Have you ever cut your own hair? How did it look?

Have you ever gotten an autograph? Whose?

Have you ever traveled by train?

Have you ever ridden on an elephant or a camel?

Have you ever ridden a horse?

Have you ever played in the rain?

Have you ever roller-skated or ice-skated?

Have you ever gone to a high school reunion?

Firsts

What was the first band or concert you went to see?

How old were you when you first moved away from home?

Do you believe in love at first sight? Have you seen it happen?

Who was running for president the first time you voted?

What was your first car?

Who was your first kiss?

What was your first big dream?

Where did you go on your first plane ride?

Where did you first see fireworks?

Who was your first friend?

Off The Cuff

If you had the chance to ride in a spaceship, would you?

If you could meet anyone in history, who would you want to meet?

Who would you choose if you could have anyone make you dinner?

Do you have a hero? Who?

If you were the leader of your country, what would you do first?

Would you rather own a jet or a houseboat?

Do you think humans will eventually live on Mars?

What incredible sight have you seen in nature?

Do you know how to swim? Who taught you?

Do you sing along with the car radio?

What do you like on your pizza?

What is your favorite season?

Have you ever run a race?

What is your favorite fruit? Vegetable?

How many hours do you sleep at night?

What would you put in a time capsule?

Who makes you laugh?

Final Questions and Prompts

Write down a list of things you enjoy.

What is a good life?

What would you like your family to know and remember?

Use this space to share more pictures, stories, and memories.

Rachel Hutcheson is a writer of funny, whimsical, and uplifting books. She also creates guided journals and other interactive books that inspire a person's creativity and imagination. You can find more of her work at: www.rachelhutchesonwriter.com

Made in the USA
Middletown, DE
29 October 2023

41483435R00064